For our husbands, Jason and Allen,
who have shown us what it means
to truly love us "in sickness and in health".
Thank you for all your
encouragement and support.

A Word from Vicki (the author)

A few years ago, I decided to concentrate on the psalms during my quiet times with God, immersing myself in just one psalm each day. I took the time to read them in several translations and to understand them on a heart level, whilst applying them to my own life. Once I had spent time meditating on them, I penned a prayer based on each psalm.

I found these prayers to be such a personal blessing and believed these should not be kept to myself, but something to be shared with others. I did this mostly through Facebook and received some good feedback. Several people commented that they would be great in a book. This book, "Pause in God's Presence: Praying the Psalms Volume 2 Psalms 76-150" and its companion book, "Pause in God's Presence: Praying the Psalms Volume 1 Psalms 1-75" is the result of both the time I spent alone in psalms and because of the encouragement I received from others.

I have self-published a previous book, "Praying Through Proverbs" which included colour photos, but this time I wanted to do something different. It was some months back I discovered my friend, Lisa, from church, had a gift for drawing and she shared her artwork on social media. I approached her to see if she would be happy to illustrate this book with her black and white illustrations. I don't think she initially realised the magnitude of the task – I wanted one illustration per prayer, which amounted to over 150 (as I had broken down Psalm 119 into several prayers)!

However, she agreed and has spent many hours creating these beautiful illustrations. She will be sharing with you a bit of her story in the next section.

When you read the Book of Psalms in the Bible, you will come across the word "Selah" or "Interlude". It appears seventy-one times in the psalms and many commentators believe it is a musical term and means "to pause or reflect". This is what I did as I read through the psalms, I would pause, reflect, and meditate on what I read. One of the Bible translations I used was The Passion Translation and instead of the word 'Selah', they used the term, 'Pause in his presence' which gave me the title for this book. What a joy and privilege it is to take time to pause and rest in God's presence and allow him to minister to our hearts, minds, and souls.

Vicki

A Word from Lisa (the illustrator)

I have always loved reading the Psalms and I tend to meditate on one a day. When Vicki approached me, I had just found out I had breast cancer and would need an operation and chemotherapy for 6 months. I have always worked full-time, loving my job as a nursery manager which I have done for eighteen years.

Before Vicki spoke to me, I had prayed to God asking him how he could use me now I couldn't work and would be at home isolating for a year. I felt very disheartened.

One day during prayer I heard him say very clearly, "Use your talents". I didn't know what to make of that but then my eyes fell on my prayer journal which was filled with doodles and drawings, and I realised that I now had the time to do my artwork (something I never had the time to do before).

My husband suggested I start to share my pictures on social media. To my utter surprise and delight, it really took off and before I knew it, I had made many Christian friends from all over the world who messaged me daily to say how my pictures inspired and helped them with God's Word.

When Vicki asked me to illustrate her book, I was beyond honoured and very excited. I knew God had his hand in it. Vicki would send me her beautiful psalm reflection which I would meditate and pray over and ask for help and guidance on how to illustrate it. Most times God would put a picture in my head, and I would prayerfully draw that image. The process was very spiritual and uplifting and distracted me from the effects of the chemotherapy. I honestly felt the Holy Spirit took over when I drew, and I felt so thoroughly blessed by God and looked after during this new phase in my life. I felt so close to God whilst I drew, and I pray you will be able to draw close to him too as you colour in the pictures.

God always has a good plan for our lives, and He has been so faithful. Even the cancer which should have caused grief led me to an unexpected year of pure joy and happiness and I am so thankful for the year I have had.

Lisa

How To Use This Book

"Pause in God's Presence" is a short meditative book. The aim of the book is to help you engage with the psalms and meditate and reflect on them prayerfully and mindfully. My written prayer may lead you into your own prayer based on that psalm. One way of using this book would be to first open your own Bible and read the psalm (or read it online) and then go on to read the accompanying prayer.

I have included Lisa's illustrations as an aid to help with your reflections and meditations on God's Word. There is the option for those of you who enjoy mindful colouring to colour in the illustrations should you wish to. You can use the illustrations as another way to connect with the psalm and meditate and reflect on it, or you can reflect on the psalm as you colour it in.

My desire is that this book will help you to take time during the day to pause in God's presence.

We lead such busy, full lives and so often we can forget to include God in our day. This is a book that will help people to connect or reconnect with God for a few moments. Now, more than ever, people need that connection with God, and I believe the recent pandemic has highlighted our need for connection and our need to stop and rest in our day.

I know over the last few years there has also been a return to Christian mindfulness and the realisation, especially in my life, that our service to God needs to overflow from our relationship with him. I believe my book will be a tool to help you to do this.

There is now also a greater understanding and awareness of mental wellbeing, and the need to care for our wellbeing. This book is one way of helping people in this area. Spending time in the psalms is a great way of helping us express our emotions in a healthy way. Reading the psalms also helps to strengthen our spiritual wellbeing.

The language I have used in my prayers is, I believe, honest and relevant, and I believe can help people to express themselves before God in their own words or by making the words of my prayers their own.

Psalm 76

Lord God,

May I never forget you are a holy God, one who is glorious and majestic, who is victorious in all you do. I bring you my reverent fear and respect because you are great. Lord, I thank you that you have made my heart your dwelling place. Help me to live a life which is honouring to you. A heart which is fully committed to you.

Amen.

You have made my

your dwelling place

Psalm 77

Lord God,

Sometimes it feels like you are keeping your distance. It seems like you have forgotten your promises to me because nothing appears to be happening. But then I remember you are a mighty, all-powerful God and that you perform great wonders. You are the God who makes a way when there appears to be no way. So, I put my trust in you and ask you to lead me as one of your sheep.

Amen.

Psalm 78

Lord God,

I set my hope on you. I remember your mighty works and your faithfulness, and I give you my heart. You are powerful to save. You are merciful and forgiving. I know I have nothing to fear because you are my Shepherd-King who has always led and guided me. I trust in you.

Amen.

You have always led and guided me

Psalm 79

Lord God,

I am in despair and brought low by my suffering. For your name's sake, won't you hear my cry? Come quickly to my side and meet my need. In your compassion, rescue and restore me.

Amen.

Psalm 80

Lord God,

My Shepherd, help me to keep following your lead. Please give me the desire and the power to keep my eyes fixed on you and live according to your will. I know you love me and chose me. You have always taken care of me. May I live aware of your face always turned towards me, smiling at me.

Amen.

You have always taken
care of me

Psalm 81

Lord God,

Thank you that when I cry out to you, you hear my prayer and answer me. I know you long for me to also have a heart which is ready and willing to hear and respond to you. Please keep my heart soft and turned to you. Give me a heart which desires to hear your voice and follow where you lead.

Amen.

I desire to hear and follow your lead

Psalm 82

Lord God,

I know what it is to feel poor, weak and needy; thank you for the comfort I have received from you. Give me eyes to see those around me who are vulnerable and helpless and who are in need of comfort too. Give me your heart for them and stir me to act with compassion.

Amen.

Psalm 83

Lord God,

Throughout history people have tried to wipe out your chosen ones, Yet each time you have acted and saved your precious people. I come to you now on behalf of my fellow believers who are suffering intense persecution. Won't you act on their behalf once again, that all may know you alone are God, Sovereign over all the earth.

Amen.

You have always acted and saved your people

Psalm 84

Lord God,

I am a pilgrim on this earth and my destination is eternity with you. I long for nothing more than my eternal home. My journey has taken me to the Valley of Weeping more than once, but you have been with me and have brought me through it. Looking back, I see now how you have blessed me in those times. Thank you for giving me the strength for this pilgrimage and for taking the journey with me.

Amen.

Looking back I see how you have blessed me

Psalm 85

Lord God,

Thank you for your many blessings to me. Thank you for your forgiveness and salvation, that you have restored me to a right relationship with you. You show me unfailing love. Your righteousness, truth, faithfulness and peace are ever with me. Thank you for the peace I experience as I follow in your ways.

Amen.

Thank you for your many

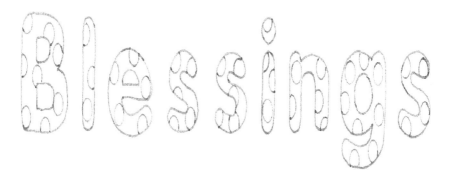

Psalm 86

Lord God,

There is none like you. You are merciful, good, forgiving, holy, unfailingly loving, faithful, compassionate and slow to anger. You are my helper, my rescuer and my comforter. I long for your help because I am poor and needy. Won't you bend your ear towards me and hear my cry? I know without a doubt that when I call out to you, you will answer me.

Amen.

Won't you bend your ear and hear my cry?

Psalm 87

Lord God,

Thank you that my name is written in your book and that my citizenship is in heaven. Thank you for blessing me with an inheritance to be enjoyed now as well as in the future. Whilst I am here on earth help me to live as a citizen of heaven.

Amen.

Thank you that my name is written in your book

Psalm 88

Lord God,

I am in such a deep, dark pit. I am overwhelmed by my pain and zapped of all my strength. My eyes are red and swollen from all my crying. My friends feel far from me and your face is hidden from me. But I'm going to keep crying out to you, day and night. I know you will hear my prayer because I trust in you, in your faithfulness and unfailing love for me.

Amen.

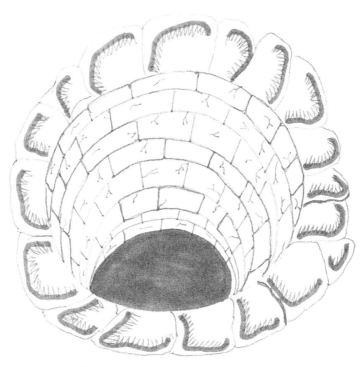

I am in such a deep, dark pit

Psalm 89

Lord God,

There is none like you, in heaven or on earth. You are the creator of all things. Your faithfulness and unfailing love last forever. You keep your word. You are a mighty ruler who rules with justice, righteousness, love and truth. When I praise and worship you, my heart is changed from doubt, fear and discouragement to joy, gratitude and hope. When I worship you, I journey in the light of your presence.

Amen.

I journey in the light of you presence

Psalm 90

Lord God,

I realise my time here on earth is short. I want to make the most of my time, doing those things you have called me to do. Please give me a heart of wisdom to know how to do this; the desire to serve you and fulfil your plans for me; the perseverance to keep going; and the power to enable me to succeed. May I sense your approval both now and when I see you face to face. I long to hear the words: "Well done, my good and faithful servant."

Amen.

I want to do those things you have called me to do

Psalm 91

Lord God,

I love you. I thank you that my life is hidden with Christ in you. You are my shelter, my refuge, my safe place. In your shadow I find rest - rest from all my fears, worries, and burdens, and you give me peace. You are the one who gives me strength to face the day. Thank you that I can live in your presence, moment by moment.

Amen.

Psalm 92

Lord God,

In the morning I praise you for your unfailing love to me and in the evening I look back on your continued faithfulness to me. Thank you for anointing me with oil for your service. May I continue to grow in grace, bear fruit and flourish in my old age.

Amen.

Psalm 93

Lord God,

In a world which is changing and uncertain, I look to you. You are seated on your throne and reign from everlasting to everlasting. You are mighty and victorious. Your throne is secure, nothing and no one can shake you, and neither can our world be shaken because you have established it. Your word is unchanging - I trust in you and your word which stands firm and true.

Amen.

I trust in you and your word

Psalm 94

Lord God,

I feel like I'm slipping. Life is so hard and my faith is weak. I am overwhelmed by worries and anxieties. I cry out to you for help. Please steady me, help me to keep standing despite what is happening around me. Thank you for the support and strength you give me. When I focus on your unfailing love for me the ground beneath my feet is firm and secure.

Amen.

The ground beneath my feet is firm and secure

Psalm 95

Lord God,

You are the mighty God, creator of all things. You watch over me as a shepherd watches over his sheep. Thank you for giving me access to your place of rest. Keep my heart soft, please Lord, may it never grow hard towards you. Then I will always willingly submit to your ways, trust you, listen to your voice and follow in obedience.

Amen.

You watch over me as a shepherd watches over his sheep

Psalm 96

Lord God,

There are always new reasons to sing praise to you. You alone are great and worthy to be praised. I worship you and bring myself as an offering to you. May my life and words be a testimony to the good news that you love each one of us and that salvation is found in you.

Amen.

Psalm 97

God,

You are Lord of the whole earth and you are Lord of my life. May you always have first place in my heart, may nothing else take your rightful place. Shine your light on the path so I can see the way you want me to take. May I not wander off and choose my own way because I know when I'm on the path you've set before me I experience such incredible joy and peace.

Amen.

Shine your light on my path

Psalm 98

Lord God,

I rejoice in your love for me. Thank you that your love is steadfast and unconditional. Thank you that nothing, not even death, can separate me from your love. Thank you for your faithfulness, you have never let me down. You remain true to your word. I trust and rejoice in the promise of Christ's return.

Amen.

Nothing can separate
me from your

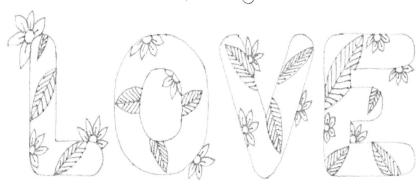

Psalm 99

Lord God,

I praise you and bow before you for you alone are holy. There is nothing of myself which is holy and yet you are willing to indwell me. Lord, help me to be holy because you are holy. May I live differently from the world and in doing so bring glory to your name.

Amen.

Psalm 100

Lord God,

Thank you that you have created me to know you. You have chosen me to belong to you, I am your prized possession. Thank you that my identity is found in you. It doesn't matter what others think of me. I can always come back to the truth that I am loved by you.

Amen.

Psalm 101

Lord God,

I desire to live a life of integrity. Would you help me as I know I can't do this on my own. Whether I am home alone or in public may I always behave and live the same, always living to please you. You have blessed me with like-minded friends. Thank you that these friends and I can encourage and support each other.

Amen.

Thank you for friends who encourage and support me

Psalm 102

Lord God,

Won't you listen to my cry? I'm discouraged and weak. It's more than I can bear right now. Are you there God? I feel abandoned and misunderstood. I'm withering away. I can't sleep and I can't eat. My body has turned against me. BUT then I remember that you, God are enthroned forever. All else will fade away, but you remain the same forever. I praise you that all your promises and purposes are fulfilled in Jesus.

Amen.

All else will fade away, but you remain the same forever

Psalm 103

Lord God,

I praise you with all that is in me - mind, heart, soul and strength. Forgive me for the times I have taken you and all you have done for me for granted. As I think on the many ways you have blessed me, I am blown away! You have forgiven me and removed my sins as far as the east is from the west. You have redeemed me and given me life. You fill my life with good things. You are a father to me, showing me unfailing love, compassion and mercy. You know me inside out and yet you continue to love me. You have given me every spiritual blessing in Christ. I praise you with all that is in me.

Amen.

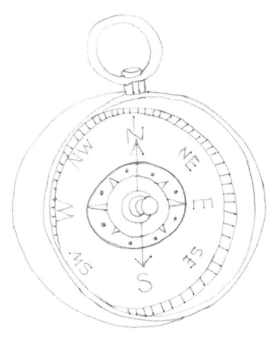

You have removed my sins as far as the east is from the west

Psalm 104

Lord God,

I marvel at your creation and your creativity. Thank you that you have blessed me with a relationship with your son, Jesus - everything was created by him and for him and he holds it all together. Thank you for my place in your creation. May I be a good steward of all you have given me.

Amen.

I marvel at your creation
and creativity

Psalm 105

Lord God,

It is you I seek and long for. I long to know and be aware of your presence moment by moment. Your promise is that those who seek you will find you. The covenant you made with your people lasts forever. By faith I will hold on to your promises even when they seem long in being fulfilled.

Amen.

Your promises last forever

Psalm 106

Lord God,

I praise you that you are a good God who has done wonderful things. Thank you that you are a merciful and gracious God. Thank you for your faithfulness to me even when I have been unfaithful to you. Forgive me when I have placed something else above you in my heart and made it an idol. Only you deserve to be first in my life. May I continually seek you as my priority. I praise you because you are God from everlasting to everlasting, whose love is unfailing. Forever you remember the covenant you made with your chosen people.

Amen.

Only you deserve first place in my life

Psalm 107

Lord God,

I give thanks to you because your faithful love is everlasting. I remember how, when I have cried out in distress, you have redeemed me. You have given me hope when my situation has seemed hopeless. When I felt lost and alone in the desert you have guided me safely through and I have found my home in you. In my dark times, imprisoned by my pain, you have set me free and brought me out. When I have rebelled against you, going my own way you have heard my cry of repentance and forgiven me. When I have experienced the storms of life you have been in the storm and have brought me to your safe haven. As I look back over my life I see evidence of your faithful love to me and I praise your name. *Amen.*

You have given me hope when life seemed hopeless

Psalm 108

Lord God,

I know that the greatest battle I face is that of the mind. I know my enemy, the Devil, seeks to bring me down. Lord, I'm often battling against depressive thoughts, worries, fears and doubts. I can't overcome them on my own. But my heart is confident in you. I know I can trust in you and your help. I know that in you is my victory.

Amen.

Psalm 109

Lord God,

Thank you that because I belong to Jesus I no longer face condemnation. I am aware that Satan is always on the prowl, and he still stands as my accuser. He seeks to bring me under condemnation by reminding me of my past sins and failures. When he does this, help me to remember that you have forgiven me and made me righteous.

Amen.

Satan is always on the prowl

Psalm 110

Lord Jesus,

You are the Royal Priest-King. You are the King of Righteousness and Peace and you sit at the right hand of God the Father. Thank you that I can come boldly before the throne of God knowing you are there interceding for me, my King and High Priest. I look forward to the day when you will have victory over your enemies and will establish your kingdom on earth.

Amen.

Psalm 111

Lord God,

I thank you for redeeming me. I was held captive by sin until you sent Jesus to pay the ransom by giving himself as a sacrifice for me. You have made an everlasting covenant with your people and nothing and no one can pluck me from your hand. I belong to you and I praise your holy name.

Amen.

You sent Jesus to pay the ransom

Psalm 112

Lord God,

My heart is confident in you. I trust and rely on you. I place my faith in you because I know you are in control. Therefore, I have nothing to fear when it comes to what may happen in the future. Whatever I face has first been father-filtered through your living hands.

Amen.

My heart is

in you

Psalm 113

Lord God,

Seated on your throne above. None can compare with you. Yet you don't keep yourself aloof from us. You see and hear us in our need and you act on our behalf. In your grace and love you sent your son, Jesus, to be one of us, to live amongst us and meet us in our need. I praise you, God.

Amen.

Psalm 114

Lord God,

You are an awesome God, a powerful God who has authority over all of creation. You removed all obstacles in the path of the Israelites as they escaped Egypt. Yet, sometimes I forget you do the same for me. You have the power to remove the obstacles which block my path so I can move in the direction you would have me take. Help me to remember that what I see as an obstacle is no obstacle to you.

Amen.

An obstacle to me is no obstacle to you

Psalm 115

Lord God,

I trust in you. My confidence is in you and your word because you are faithful and true. I find refuge in you as I cling to you. You are my help and shield.

Amen.

You are my help and shield

Psalm 116

Lord God,

That you should want to hear my voice is such an amazing truth and one I sometimes struggle to believe. That you should bend your ear to listen is a precious thought. Thank you for giving me your undivided attention. Oh, that I would be the same when you speak to me.

Amen.

You give me you undivided attention

Psalm 117

Lord God,

I praise you because of your unfailing love and faithfulness. You are always true to yourself and to your word. I place my faith and trust in you.

Amen.

I praise you for your unfailing love

Psalm 118

Lord God,

I place my faith in you. You are my security. I may look for security in other things such as my health, finance, home, possessions or people, but these things are fleeting and temporary. Real security can only be found in you. You, O God, are always with me and you are always on my side. Therefore, I have nothing to fear.

Amen.

You are always on my side,
you are my security

Psalm 119:1-16

Lord God,

I love you and your word more than anything. I long to know you better and love you more. Help me to treasure your word in my heart. Teach me your ways that I will live according to your instruction and know true joy. Thank you that you never give up on me, even when I do wander off your path.

Amen.

Psalm 119:17-40

Lord God,

When I come to your word, I ask that you would give me spiritual understanding. Would you reveal the truth to me and give me insight. I ask for a teachable heart and a willingness to learn. I want to not only understand your truths, I want them to have an impact on my day to day life. That I might be guided by them and receive direction for the path you set before me.

Amen.

Give me a teachable heart and a willingness to learn

Psalm 119:41-88

Lord God,

Your word is full of promises you have made to your people and to me. Remember the promises you have made; they are my hope and they comfort me. I seek out your promises and I hold on to them as I wait for your timing. Help me to wait with hope and as I wait, help me to walk in obedience. Then I will have a wonderful testimony to share with others.

Amen.

I seek out
and hold onto your

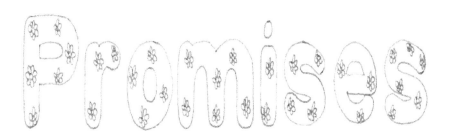

Psalm 119:89-120

Lord God,

I will meditate on your word continually. Your word is sweeter than honey. I love to eat from it, chew it over and digest it. Your word is my greatest treasure. As I meditate you give me joy, life, guidance, wisdom, understanding and hope. Your word becomes part of my life as my meditations lead to obedient action.

Amen.

Psalm 119:121-144

Lord God,

I thank you for your word. Thank you that I don't need to wait for someone else to explain it to me. You are the greatest teacher, so I come before you as I open my Bible and ask that you would reveal its truths to me. Your word brings spiritual insight and guidance. Please give me the ability to learn and a teachable heart so that I understand what you are saying to me and how to apply it to my day-to-day life.

Amen.

Psalm 119:145-160

Lord God,

Your word is absolute truth. Your word never changes. When all else fades away, your word remains. Your word and your Spirit bring me life, they strengthen and encourage me. I fix my mind on your word. It's your word which brings me hope.

Amen.

It's your word that brings me hope

Psalm 119:161-176

Lord God,

I experience such joy as I dig into the treasures of your word and as you reveal them to me. They are treasures of eternal value and exceed all earthly treasure. As I take joy in your word, I am filled with such an incredible sense of peace, well-being, wholeness, satisfaction and contentment. Thank you, Lord.

Amen.

I dig into the treasures of your word

Psalm 120

Lord God,

When I'm faced with troubles I can quickly turn to worrying. I try to fix things myself, but this only leads to feeling overwhelmed by it all. Help me to come to you first with my troubles and cry out to you. In the past, when I've done that, you have answered me and restored my peace. It is this past experience which gives me confidence to cry out to you today.

Amen.

I come to you with my troubles

Psalm 121

Lord God,

As I journey through this life thank you that you watch over me, that you guard and protect me and keep me safe from harm. You keep me close to you. You watch over every detail of my life, all my comings and my goings. What comfort and peace that gives me.

Amen.

As I journey, you watch over me

Psalm 122

Lord God,

I thank you that you have brought like-minded people into my life that we might journey together, giving encouragement and support to each other. When I fall down may a fellow companion stop to help me up. When another is finding the journey hard may I encourage them to keep going. When there is joy on the way may we celebrate together. As we journey help us to fix our eyes on you and our ultimate destination, worshipping you along the way.

Amen.

Friends journey together

Psalm 123

Lord God,

I choose to fix my eyes on you, the one who rules above it all. I hand my problems over to you and trust you with them because you are God and I am not. I will fix my eyes on Jesus, the author and perfecter of my faith.

Amen.

Psalm 124

Lord God,

When I look back over my life, the trials and difficulties I have been through, I don't know how I would have survived had it not been for your being there for me. Had you not been on my side I don't know where I would be today. I thank you for being an ever-present constant in my life. Thank you, mighty God for being my helper and defender.

Amen.

Psalm 125

Lord God,

In you alone is my security, I trust in you, you are my firm foundation. Jesus Christ is my solid rock, on whom I build my life. You, O God, enable me to stand firm when the circumstances of life threaten to shake me.

Amen.

Jesus Christ, my solid rock

Psalm 126

Lord God,

There are times when life is hard and I struggle to do the things you call me to do. Times when I'd rather curl up in a ball under the bedcovers and let my tears flow. But you call me to still be faithful and serve you despite my tears. Help me, Lord, to do the next thing even when I don't feel like it. I thank you for your promise that even though I may be sad right now and sow in tears, there will come a day when I will rejoice in the harvest.

Amen.

One day I will rejoice in the harvest

Psalm 127

Lord God,

There was a time when what I did for you was all in my own strength, I worked hard and was over-confident in myself. But this led to exhaustion. You graciously showed me this is not how you wanted me to live. You have taught me that apart from you I can do nothing. Now I work with you and rely on your strength. You teach me how to enjoy the balance between work and rest.

Amen.

Psalm 128

Lord God

I've known the joy of loving you from childhood and this has been such a blessing to me. Thank you for my husband who is another of your blessings to me. As we grow closer as a couple may we together grow closer to you. Thank you for blessing us with our children. May our relationship with you be an example to them. If you grant us the blessing of grandchildren may our lives continue to be a testimony of your goodness. My desire is for each member of my family to know and love you as I do.

Amen.

Psalm 129

Lord God,

Following you is not always easy. I have known the weariness of battle and been overwhelmed by pressures, but never been totally crushed. I have been discouraged but never without hope. Rejected by others but never abandoned by you. Knocked down but I've got up again. I'm still standing because you are with me. Your Holy Spirit gives me the inner strength I need to persevere. In spite of it all, I can still say with confidence, YOU ARE GOOD!

Amen.

I am still standing because you are with me

Psalm 130

Lord God,

I'm in such a low place right now, hear my cry and save me. I'm counting on you, Lord. I will wait with patient expectation, knowing you will answer my cry. I put my hope in you and in your word.

Amen.

Psalm 131

Lord God,

Being spiritually weaned by you is initially a painful experience and not a process I've enjoyed. But I see now you have weaned me off certain things for my good and to bring me to spiritual maturity. It has freed me to find rest and contentment in you.

Amen.

Psalm 132

Lord God,

That you should choose to indwell me is mind blowing. You have made my heart your home and have promised to remain there forever. What peace this brings me. Yet, I am challenged by it too. May my life, everything I say and do, reflect the truth that you dwell in me.

Amen.

Psalm 133

Lord Jesus,

Your prayer for those who believe in you is that we will be one as you and the Father are one. There is unity when we allow the Holy Spirit to have his way. Help us to focus more on what we have in common, than on our differences. How beautiful is the sound we all make when we live in harmony with one another, just like an orchestra when each one plays their part.

Amen.

What a beautiful sound

Psalm 134

Lord God,

Sometimes sleep does not come easily to me. I wake during the night and have difficulty falling back to sleep. I toss and turn, unable to switch off my mind. Worries consume me and my problems keep me awake as I search for a solution. Help me to remember when I have trouble sleeping to focus on you. You are with me and you never sleep. Instead of worrying, I can turn my mind to praising you and fixing my thoughts on you.

Amen.

You are
with me
night
and day

Psalm 135

Lord God,

Whilst others may see me as insignificant, you have chosen me to be your treasured possession. I am special to you. What an incredible thing it is to be chosen and loved by you. Help me to live my life as your treasured possession. May knowing how you feel about me shape my attitudes and my actions.

Amen.

I am your treasured possession

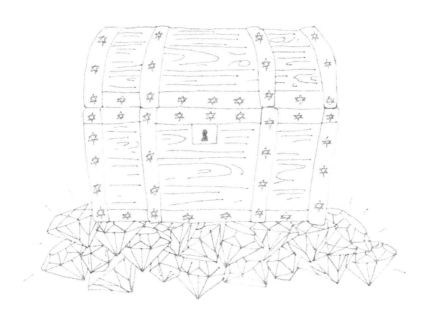

Psalm 136

Lord God,

I praise you for the grace, mercy and compassion you have shown me and continue to show me. Your faithful love endures forever. You have redeemed me by the precious blood of your son, Jesus Christ. You lead me safely on my earthly journey. I praise you for your faithful love endures forever.

Amen.

Your faithful love endures forever

Psalm 137

Lord God,

I come to you to express my grief and the pain of my loss. When I tried to ignore it, dismiss it or keep it buried I was not dealing with it in a healthy way. I was held captive by my body and my mind. But you have brought freedom to my spirit and soul. Help me to act and live and move in this freedom.

Amen.

Psalm 138

Lord God,

Thank you that you had a plan for my life even before I was born. I had plans for my life, yet I have found your plans to be better than mine. Thank you that you are the one who will accomplish them. I don't need to strive to make them happen. Help me trust you as you work them out and as I partner with you.

Amen.

Psalm 139

Lord God,

You know everything there is to know about me. You know me inside out. You know my thoughts, words and actions. You are with me and have been with me even before I was born. You know exactly who I am and yet you love me as one who is most precious to you. I can do no better in my life than to follow where you lead because your plans for me are good and right.

Amen.

Psalm 140

Lord God,

I thank you that you have saved me and none can pluck me from your hand. Yet, this doesn't stop Satan from trying to bring me down and cause me to stumble. I recognise that he often tries to attack my mind, to cause me to doubt you and believe his lies. I cry out to you and ask that you would protect my mind during battle because you are my strong Saviour.

Amen.

Psalm 141

Lord God,

Would you keep a guard over my mouth because it's impossible for me to tame my tongue on my own. Help me to think before I speak. May I store up good things in my heart because I know it's from the overflow of my heart that I speak. When others correct me for my good and to encourage my spiritual maturity, help me to respond and accept it graciously.

Amen.

Psalm 142

Lord God,

I'm in a dark place, I can't see any light at the end and I see no way out. My spirit is weak. So, I'm pouring out my heart to you, telling you of all my troubles. Please, won't you let me know that you've heard me? I know you are the only safe place for me. You are all I have and you are all I need.

Amen.

You are the only safe place for me

Psalm 143

Lord God,

Hear my prayer and answer me. I'm in a deep depression and my hope is fading. Show yourself to me because I can't live without you. Show me what to do and lead me forward. Help me to keep going even when the going is tough.

Amen.

Help me to keep going

Psalm 144

Lord God,

You are my tower of strength, my deliverer, my protector and the one in whom I take refuge. It never ceases to amaze me that a great God like you should care to know and love me, and that I am always on your mind. When I think about who you are and all you have done it causes me to break out with a new song of praise.

Amen.

Psalm 145

Lord God,

You are an awesome God and I meditate on your greatness. You are righteous, compassionate, gracious, slow to anger and abounding in love. You keep your promises. All my needs are met in you. I have so many reasons to praise you and tell of your greatness. There is always something new for me to discover about you.

Amen.

You keep your promises

Psalm 146

Lord God,

My confidence and hope is in you, the Eternal King, not in people who are here one day and gone the next. You who made heaven and earth are here for us all. You show compassion, grace, mercy and love to the weak, the vulnerable, the helpless and the lonely. I will praise you all the days of my life.

Amen.

You show compassion to all

Psalm 147

Lord God,

Thank you for being close to me in my pain and caring about what I have suffered. Thank you for binding my wounds and healing the sorrow of my heart. Thank you that you are making something beautiful from my brokenness. May I never be ashamed of my scars because they are evidence of your healing work in me.

Amen.

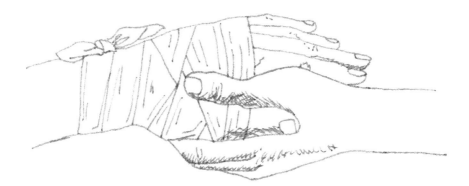

Psalm 148

Lord God,

You are the great I AM. You are the only one worthy of my praise. My constant, close friend, unchanging one. The whole earth joins together in an orchestra of praise - the sun, moon, stars, creatures of the sky, sea and land, the mountains, valleys and trees. We all praise your name.

Amen.

Psalm 149

Lord God,

I love to gather with my church family to worship you and sing your praises. I know how much you delight in our worship. But there are times when I don't have the strength to leave my bed, however much I long to be with my church. Yet I can use the time to listen to worship music even if I have no voice. I can meditate on you even when I cannot read my Bible. I can rest in you. I am learning I can glorify you from the confines of my bedroom. You delight in me.

Amen.

Psalm 150

Lord God,

You are the one who has given me breath and I will use it to sing my praises to you. I will make a joyful noise because it arises from an attitude of worship for all you are and for all you have done. My praise delights your heart and I will continue to praise you.

Amen.

I will use my breath to sing your praises

About the Author

I live in Eastbourne, in the South East of England. I am married to Jason, we have two adult children, and one dog, Rue.

God has blessed me with a love for His Word, for studying it and sharing it with others. I enjoy teaching from His Word and helping others to see how it relates to their lives in the 21st Century. He has also given me a joy for writing and sharing His Word through my writing.

If you would like to connect with me, you can do so via:
- My website: www.vickicottingham.com
- Facebook: @VickiCottinghamWriter
- Instagram: @VickiCottingham

My other books:
- Dear Friend…Volume 1 & 2 (Each book has 52 weekly devotions to encourage, challenge and inspire)
- Praying Through Proverbs: Fresh, reflective and helpful everyday prayers inspired from the book of Proverbs

- An Advent Devotional: Hope, Faith, Joy and Love & Worship

These books are all available through Amazon or by contacting me directly.

About the Illustrator

I live in Eastbourne with my husband, Allen, and my many animals. I am a great animal lover.

I have run a Catholic nursery school for over fifteen years and have always loved using art to illustrate stories for the children and using art for teaching.

If you would like to get in contact with me or would like an individual sketch or commission piece, please email lisasimmonds80@hotmail.com

For my Instagram page please go to pugspraiseandpictures

Printed in Great Britain
by Amazon